Fear & Faith

ANDRÉ LODRÉE JR.

Copyright © 2015 André Lodrée Jr.

All rights reserved. No part of this book may be reproduced, stored, or transmitted by any means—whether auditory, graphic, mechanical, or electronic—without written permission of both publisher and author, except in the case of brief excerpts used in critical articles and reviews. Unauthorized reproduction of any part of this work is illegal and is punishable by law.

Contents

FAITH

Fear

Alone

1 Corinthians 15:31(*KJV*)

Accomplishments made, goals reached
Successful career, no time for sleep
Went through it all
Through every leap and fall
Became more than my dream
I'm my own team
A citizen of trans world
Secrets unfurled
Unlimited power
People are like a flower
Beautiful one day
The next thrown away
Life is unmatched
No itch can't be scratched
The keys to the kingdom
With authority to run
I've arrived with no invitations
Greeted with the host's apologies & exceptions
Smiles for everyone
People in my presence know how to have fun
I'm the king
That wants for nothing
That needs everything
That can obtain anything
You see me every day in your dreams
Your grass is brown and mine is green
You spend money and time on me

Because you hope I will set you free
No more mundane
No more sane
Free to be crazy
Or to enjoy a day of lazy
Pure indulgence
Makes pure sense

So here we are alone
Fighting with all our muscles and bones
To get closer to each other

Horror Story

"But the day of the Lord will come like a thief. The heavens will disappear with a roar; the elements will be destroyed by fire, and the earth and everything in it will be laid bare."

2 Peter 3:10 (*NIV*)

Have you ever seen the sunshine on a rainy day, I have
I've seen a tree stand in the middle of a hurricane
A woman had twelve kids at one time, O the pain
Have you ever seen a man ten feet tall, I have
But as I glare at this
I am left speechless

My eyes blink in disbelief
My mind thought to speak
My throat filled with saliva
Can't even scream mama
But it is too late this disaster is upon me
I'm in captivity

I blame myself because I saw it coming
And never even thought of running
I froze watching it slowly come towards me
Being hypnotized by its movement as if I couldn't see
Palms sweaty, mind racing, adrenaline pumping but body still
Amazed at the fact that this was unreal
I became a character in a horror movie
Bound by my duty
To stand and accept my fate
With tears of fear streaming down my face
As he got closer I began to recognize him
And I had heard his story from many men

He was born in a state of controversy
Wrapped in Satan's mercy
His family was hunted and chased out of town
And now his home can no longer be found
His murder has been told and heard by plenty
For years they terrorized his family
Even though he has been dead and long gone
Many even believe he lives on
They have seen him shocking this world
Chasing after young boys and girls
He has been credited for killing millions
From Chicagoans to Sicilians
Once he has you in his grasp you can never escape death
He moves like winter breath
Never being heard, but constantly happening
With each calculated step continuously attacking
Paralyzing your body with his dare
Snatching every care
And here I was engulfed in his presence
Tied up in His murderous excellence

Children

"Do you hear what these children are saying?" they asked him. "Yes," replied Jesus, "have you never read, "'From the lips of children and infants you have ordained praise'?"

Matthew 21:16 (*NIV*)

To open the door of the past opens the lives of the future
With every subject we tutor
Our children about their century
From the books, classes and homework of high school and elementary
We show them who they are going to be
Teaching them how to do math and how not to repeat history
But are they listening to our words?
Or are they protecting their minds with shields and swords
Simultaneously rejecting the past and destroying the future
Just to enjoy everything sooner
Give them calculators to keep them from using their minds
Give them digital clocks so they don't know how to tell time
Give them television with supposed news information
Give them reality shows to destroy their imagination
Tell them mediocre is average
Tell them they'll never do better so they ignore the message
Show them doing wrong can bring success
And now they will never try their best

Who will stand?
Who will give them a new plan?
Who will say they can change?
Who will teach them how to speak English and not just slang?
Who will turn off the television and hand them a book?
Who will unplug the microwave and teach them how to cook?

Who will show them love and not lust?
Who will stop the lies and develop their trust?
Who will instruct them how to be a sister or brother?
Who will stop the baby making and develop fathers and mothers?

Can our culture continue with such negative perpetuation?
Can our children destroy our horrific infatuation?
Or will this continue until the present becomes the future
And then we'll be the loser
So we must reset, repair, reconstruct
And stop depending on luck
They'll understand, life will teach them
But with no defense can they win
We can't say we can't teach nothing
They know everything
Sure we can't start to teach at age thirteen
By now they have developed their dream
And our encouraging words cannot fit between the seams
Don't think they're grown and treat them mean
Frustration has caused us to curse our descendants
Forcing them to independency when they are still infants

Yet who will stand?
Who will give them a new plan?
Who will write the vision and make it plain?
No one's running instead the lack of a plan is driving us insane?

Family

"If anyone does not provide for his relatives, and especially for his immediate family, he has denied the faith and is worse than an unbeliever."

1 Timothy 5:8 (NIV)

When I was born into this world I was given a family
People that were ordained to love and care for me
They were given authority over me
To show me what God wanted me to be
God gave them the tools to raise and develop me
Love, compassion, respect, community, discipline & reciprocity

So I came into this world with hope
That my family would not be a bunch of dopes
I knew their love would over power every ounce of fear & doubt
I knew their compassion would understand my cries & shouts
I knew their respect would protect me from any mental, verbal, phys-
      ical or sexual abuse
I knew their community would give me that encouraging boost
I knew their discipline would prepare me for life success
I knew their reciprocity would show me to only accept an
      individual's best
But now that I'm here I wonder where these things went
I wonder why I was sent
I wonder why family ignores the tools given to them by God
Is it me am I just too odd
Do I cry too much
Do I talk too much
Do I ask too many questions
Am I too dependent on their protection
Am I too curious

Am I too serious
Do I need too much love
Or do they treat me this way just because

When I was born into this world I was given a family
People that were ordained to love and care for me
They were given authority over me
To show me what God wanted me to be
Blessed with the tools to raise and develop me
Love, compassion, respect, community, discipline & reciprocity

Where are these tools?
Have you let you cause me to lose?

The Fall From The Tree

"Then Jesus said to his disciples, "If anyone would come after me, he must deny himself and take up his cross and follow me."

Matthew 16:24 (*NIV*)

Coming to a point of change
Makes life strange
I have tried not to conform
But in every instance my stance is the norm
My individuality is lost in space
Because someone has already sat in my place
I can never move on my own
I'm not a king on a throne
I'm not God but his subject
I'm not the power but the reset
A number among the masses
I'm not the smartest, tallest or fastest
The apple does not fall far from the tree
If this is true where's my identity

I feel more average than extraordinary
Not too brave, I'm mostly scary
More interested in running than fighting
More interested in reading than writing
Can't endure anything without crying
Can't tell the truth because of lying
With ambitions of being great
I found myself holding the hand of hate
Despising those that are famous
Only because I felt I was nameless
The apple does not fall far from the tree
If this is true where's my identity

Laying here on the grass only looking at the other apples, I'm hypnotized
Watching the sunrise
And shining on the other apples' skin
Causing the apples to gleam with beauty, but what's within
Underneath their skin are the apples rotten with no seeds?
How can I follow their lead?
I changed my perspective and I looked up
I couldn't see anything because of all the green stuff
There it was the tree that created me
But could I become the tree?

Reward

"For the scripture saith, Thou shalt not muzzle the ox that treadeth out the corn. And, The labourer is worthy of his reward."

1 Timothy 5:18 (*KJV*)

What is the reward
For leaning on my lord?
What is the benefit
For His spirit?

Have you accepted Jesus as your savior?
I'm tired of these church haters
Interrupting my life with this stuff
Man enough is enough
I love my life
I love kicking it every night
I enjoy dancing and drinking
I'm tired of hearing my parents say – Are you thinking?
I want it all
Ball till I fall

What is the reward
For leaning on my lord?
What is the benefit
For His spirit?

I look at these church people
They don't have nothing but a steeple
Long skirts
Ties & shirts
In the bed by 10

Talking about Jesus is my friend
They never even seen this dude
Probably reading this saying – He's so rude
But God still loves him
And forgives every sin
Always talking about you headed to hell
Can't you tell

What is the reward
For leaning on my lord?
What is the benefit
For His spirit?

I don't need the Holy Ghost
I'm the host with the most
The life of the party
Me stop, hardly
I got too much going on
Being a Christian – yawn
I'm straight
God can wait

What is the reward
For leaning on my lord?
What is the benefit
For His spirit?

Where was God when my father left?
Where was God when my grandparents met death?
My mother alone with three kids
Trivial men putting in bogus husband bids
Using her & moving on to the next one
Guaranteed promises, but ending up with none
My sisters never learned about men
So to please them they thought they had to indulge in sin

Now I'm a twenty year old uncle
Thinking in less than twenty years I could be a granduncle
There ain't no room in my life for God
So I'll enjoy my life just the way it is flawed

What is the reward
For leaning on my lord?
What is the benefit
For His spirit?

Destiny

"This day I call heaven and earth as witnesses against you that I have set before you life and death, blessings and curses. Now choose life, so that you and your children may live."

Deuteronomy 30:19 (*NIV*)

It has become very difficult to live on
Knowing that my life has been filled with wrongs
I have enjoyed life to the fullest
My actions have been focused on the coolest
I have structured my life around marketing campaigns
My best friends are those who never refrained
Always willing to risk it all on a moment
But my roller coaster was missing a component
I could not find the answer to my mystery
And my life slowly became history

New moved to old
For sale became sold
And there I was at the center of attention
Enjoying my fallible retention
Accepting my mistakes as virtues
But steadily given the opportunity to choose
I took the hand off and ran straight into a pile on
Kept dropping back and never looking long
Never thinking I can gain instead of lose
Changing the channel when I saw my news
I had a choke hold on me
Never trying to escape because I was free

But there comes a time in everyone's life when our responses are redundant
Finally being stuck in a revolving door becomes repugnant
At that point we look to exit or enter
But our senses brings fear of the winter
Because we would rather be stuck in a circle of fire
Then sit in the cold till the winter retires
Blind to the future causes total obedience to the present
So we can't afford the mortgage and enjoy the rent
We focus on everyday travel instead of everyday living
We are the greatest borrowers so how can we be giving

The Gift

"Peace I leave with you; my peace I give you. I do not give to you as the world gives. Do not let your hearts be troubled and do not be afraid."

John 14:27 (*NIV*)

There it is right before my eyes
Has Jesus given me a chance to rise?
Rise above this society of distrust
A world with eyes of lust
Has he blessed me like this?
With such a beautiful gift

A gift with a special touch of love
A gift sent from above
A gift unknown to many, seen by few
A gift designed, blueprinted, for you

Not me, I am not worthy of God's blessing
My life, my ways, my thoughts have not pleased Him
As I stand in disbelief and incomprehension
Yet I alone admire this gift of love and precision
Has He blessed me like this?
With such a beautiful gift

Stand Still

"If a man dies, will he live again? All the days of my struggle I will wait Until my change comes."

Job 14:14 (*NAS*)

People change
We grow
We know
We live
We give
We try
We die
We reach
We teach
We build
We feel
People change

Our connections are deep
We have the same amount of hands and feet
We bleed the same color blood
We all give some kind of love
We each have a mother and a father
Sometimes we don't feel like being bothered
We all have attitudes
Occasionally we can't help but be rude
We have stories and feelings that we don't want to share
We have our favorite outfit that we love to wear

People change
We fight
We bite
We cry

We lie
We sleep
We speak
We run
We have fun
We think
We blink
People change

You feel it every day the need for change
But then you discover that a difference is out of your range
But you steady strive for it with every fiber of your being
But changing is more than just seeing
It is believing that you can do
That you can make it through
That you can fly without wings
That you cannot sweat the small things
Every action should be moving towards this change but it's not
And that causes our vision to rot
In an effort to keep the dream fresh
We take the hands of mess
And we go backwards instead of forward
Our motivation becomes stagnant and bored
But our goal is still there
But it is no longer a double dare
It's not a feather in our cap
But a monkey on our back
Dragging us down
Beating us to the ground
So fear becomes our temporary fix
And we fall for the distraction tricks
Then we are there, where we don't want to be
But can we ever be free
Can we ever get out the grasp of fears?
Can we cut ourselves with courageous shears?
Or is a stand still our future

Hard Drive

*"I have told you these things, so that in me you may
have peace. In this world you will have trouble. But
take heart! I have overcome the world."*

John 16:33 (*NIV*)

I take two steps forward
At the same time I take three steps backward
I'm stuck in a revolving door
It's over I can't take it any more

I'm tired of living in this optical illusion
I'm tired of my life being full of confusion
I got to get myself together
But if I keep depending on me I'm going to be like this forever
Stuck in a whirlwind of empty pleasures
Defining myself with other people's measures
If only I could erase my mind like a computer hard drive
Re-teach myself how to survive
Input new fields of data and information
Allowing every key typed to develop better modifications
With each document saved
I process a better way for me to behave
With each file ran
I open a new program
That will improve who I am without a flaw
But even computers are trapped underneath imperfection's claw
Forgetting how to shut down or reboot
Being dropped on someone's front stoop
Erasing a much needed file
Realizing my life can not be saved in a folder of denial

So what can I do to get out of this repetitive cycle?
Keep myself from ingesting Dayquil and Nyquil
Walking through this life like a zombie
Enjoying fads that make me content with being phony
God has blessed me with two cheeks
And two feet
So now I have to decide what to do
I can't keep walking backwards and leave my life up to you

Next Level

"My people are destroyed for lack of knowledge: because thou hast rejected knowledge, I will also reject thee, that thou shalt be no priest to me: seeing thou hast forgotten the law of thy God, I will also forget thy children."

Hosea 4:6 (*KJV*)

Ignorance is bliss
Too much knowledge is a risk
I just want to be rich
Millions of dollars is my only wish
School is not for me
I want to get a job make some money and be free
I have dreams and goals
And school is getting old
I just want to have fun
I know enough already, I ain't dumb

Excuses, Excuses, Excuses
Words that have become abusive
We have beaten ourselves with lies
And thrown away a priceless prize
We have laughed at those who have tried to pursue it
Only because we thought we could not do it
We've looked in the mirror and seen a movie star, TV star
Sports star, rap star, R& B star
Not knowing our perceptions were wrong
Those artists don't make more than fifty cents off one song
We try to become them by imitating what we have seen and heard
Only to look up and see our bosses were our class nerds

But here we are standing, sitting, walking, and living
Trying to pursue a dream without knowing and forgetting
The tools needed to become our dream
Playing life's game without enough players on our team
But how can we go on like this
Trying to blow down houses made of bricks
But we are not here because we are oppressed
We are here because we are blessed
We are free to choose knowledge or ignorance
Free to choose subjection or independence
Each choice defines our life
Trying to decipher what's wrong or right
But how can we make the right choice with no education
How can we move to the next level with no graduation?
Freedom is education's prize
There's just one thing left to do open our eyes

Manna

Exodus 16:34-35 (*NIV*)

Many have tried but only a few succeed
They desire things that can never supply their need
Holding hands with statues
So they can never accept good news
Their ears are closed to everything that's godly
So their eyes only see probably
They don't know that God is guaranteed
So the flesh they continue to feed

I wish I could give u a happy ending
But their lives are captivated by the menu
And their lives are never in order
So they reorder & reorder until there is no porter
Love does not save them from their inaction
But hate gives them a mummified reaction
So they sit at the table with pictures of food
Oooin & ahhin about I want to try this, it looks real good
Their pallet will never enjoy the indescribable tastes
They will never know how it feels to really eat in this place
They will never know how the food strengthens
They will never know how the cook created such delicious inventions
They will never experience how abnormal spices mix under fire
They will never know how it feels to eat & then retire

Can you see anyone doing this?
If not why continue to grant Satan's wish?
Ignoring manna from on high
To indulge in drugs, sex, delinquencies and lies

Trash

*"For Jehovah hath comforted Zion; he hath com-
forted all her waste places, and hath made her wil-
derness like Eden, and her desert like the garden of
Jehovah; joy and gladness shall be found therein,
thanksgiving, and the voice of melody."*

Isaiah 51:3 (*ASV*)

For years I looked at the cover to judge the book
The inside never has enough bait on its hook
Outside is the most important not inside
And so began my life's roller coaster ride
Jumping in covenants because it looked good
Once I was in platinum, it was turned to wood
I can't believe how slow I was
Can't believe how blind I was
I couldn't understand why things weren't working
For the outside beauty I continued flirting
I was holding disaster's hand for protection
Ignorant to my allegiance to material subjection
If I was to be successful a change would have to occur
But to change meant war
Cutting off my alliance with the enemy
Would destroy him and me
Nobody can describe the affects of such devastation
However the only way to my peace was my annihilation

Confused and happy I began this battle
Like a farmer's kid daring to knock over a cattle
I dared to kill myself
Destroying the greed of power and wealth
As I began to take out the trash I did not realize how high it piled up

Mountains and hills of ignorant stuff
Negative perceptions, years of rejections
Wasted time, instance of moral crimes
Cultivating a life of pain
Dismissing joy to bask in a life of shame
Hiding behind everybody else that does it
Forcing myself to love it
But now I have opened a door that can't be closed
And throw out things that only God knows

However, I can't dismiss it all
Instead I must utilize it all
Take the trash and make it recyclable
Change incapability to capable
Allow my pain and sorrow to become my joy
Tap into my real McCoy
Search not just for love for the world, but love for me
Use discipline and restraint to be free
Embrace the little pain to be overwhelmed with unexplainable peace
Living life while keeping love in arm's reach
So now I change subtraction to addition
Use my trash to make my decisions

Letting Go

Casting all your care upon him; for he careth for you.

1 Peter 5:7 (*NIV*)

I wish I could tell you the way I feel
About my life and my pain it sometimes makes me feel unreal
But I struggle, I fight
For the next challenge, the next step with all my might
I watch as people pass me by wondering when I'll get my turn
But yet I'm here with only one thing on my mind wanting to learn
Wanting to be better than I was before
Wanting to overcome mistakes with every inch, with every pore
I try to change
I try to be more than just a lame
That's inefficient, all faculties not working
A limp leg, a limp arm only leads to me jerking
Trying to force myself to the next level
Only to find out that this life is not only base and treble
It's time for me to be loud
And proud
It's time for me to stand
With optimism in my hand
With enemies all around me
It's time for me to be me
It's time for my mind to stop wondering what I will become
To stop wondering about having some
I want to be I, because I'm tired of being you
I'm tired and I'm through
Measuring up to a fantasy
That's made me cuddle insanity
So I'll climb this mountain, I'll climb this tree

I'll go into this valley
All in the effort just to be me
It's not easy, it's not hard
But for some estrange reason I continue to play the wrong card
So can I end it all?
Can I really set myself free from this free fall?
I don't know
More importantly I don't want to know
I don't want to care
I don't want to dwell on each of life's snares
I guess it's time for me just to do
The simple thing that I should have done a long time ago
Forget what I know or don't know
And just let go

Senses

*"Oh, taste and see that the Lord is good! Blessed is
the man who takes refuge in him!"*

Psalm 34:8 (*ESV*)

If I can hear your voice in the wind
If I can feel your love in the air
If I can see your touch in the sky
Then I can know that you care

Our senses seem to limit us
And we project these limitations on Jesus
We never saw Him ascend into the sky
So He did just die
No resurrection with all power
So our senses devour
His life's ministry and His sacrificial death
His love was not shown with His every breath
His words used to challenge our traditions
And remove evil's afflictions
Are just merely absurd
And His life, I mean myth, never occurred

If I can hear your voice in the wind
If I can feel your love in the air
If I can see your touch in the sky
Then I can know that you care

We have accepted lies
Because we could not see with our eyes
We need to put our fingers through the holes to believe it's real
But blessed are they that don't need to feel

To believe that Jesus is Lord and Savior
So we allow sinful habits to develop our behavior
We're running around a race track
Chasing a phony rabbit and never stopping to look back
To see what this opportunity costs
Maybe because we're afraid to see our soul lost
So our outer garment gives us our identity
Forced to live life with no serenity

If I can hear your voice in the wind
If I can feel your love in the air
If I can see your touch in the sky
Then I can know that you care

We blindly sign contracts saying we know what we're doing
But our allies are on the sideline booing
Screaming bad decision
That's going to lead to a negative conclusion
But we fall deaf to their suggestions
Now our senses are used for our subjection
So how can we take our senses and conclude
That Jesus is just some ordinary dude
How can we love this flesh?
When the only thing can come out of it is death

If I can hear your voice in the wind
If I can feel your love in the air
If I can see your touch in the sky
Then I can know that you care
But I can't see, I can't feel
I can't hear, but I know you're real

The Secret

"A word was secretly brought to me, my ears caught a whisper of it."

Job 4:12 (*NIV*)

If we take this day to give thanks
Take a moment not to be concerned with power or rank
Stop what we're doing and enjoy life's virtue
Take one second to be true to you
Stop folding and cutting ourselves to fit the canvas of the norm
Convert to our convictions and choose not to conform
We have become trapped in an out of body experience
Convinced ourselves that our personality is a nuisance
Subjection has become our parents and leads us through this universe
Whispering do what I say before you end up in a hearse
If we take the master's whip on our backs
How will we have the strength to attack?
We have no control over time
Time causes us all to remain in line
We can have all the money and power, but can't change time
So drunk with ambition we can't see the road signs
Telling us – do not enter, stop, slow down
But we continue on going to town
Moving with the rhythm of life
But never listening to the words of life
We drink and inhale the pleasures of life
Only to rapidly discover the end of life

But before the end is near there is a foreshadow
The secrets have been released through a small window
Many have heard and read, but rejected
Some have searched the words and actions and accepted

How can we look a gift horse in the mouth?
Continue to sail north when the wind is blowing south
With each moment seeing each prophecy being fulfilled
Holding on to lies to dismiss the real
But yet it flew through a window and was grounded on a tree
Sitting in plain view for all to see
But the leaves grew and the tree got taller
And to get a glimpse has become harder and harder
But the secret still remains
And maybe that's what's driving us insane

I Got A Feeling

"But without faith it is impossible to please Him, for he who comes to God must believe that He is, and that He is a rewarder of those who diligently seek Him."

Hebrews 11:6 (*NKJV*)

I seem to be stuck in concrete
Longing for the sweet savor of victory but only tasting defeat
I know my actions are the primary causation
For this tormenting situation
But yet I'm going to blame somebody else for a bit
Just until this problem becomes a fit
Like a perfect suit I'll wear it like a model
Then my ego won't even bother
Trying to explain away my hand in this dilemma
And then I'll remember
That I'm no longer moving forward but frozen in time
Looking for a way to fight for what's rightfully mine

I got a feeling

Stationary, as life passes me by
Looking at everyone's green grass wondering why
Thinking what have I done to deserve such a tragedy?
My life's an utter disappointing catastrophe
Defined by one mistake
That will haunt me until the wake
It will become the adjective on my tombstone
The fact that will prove me wrong
To even think of overcoming is futile
So pain and tears permanently hide my smile

But I got a feeling

With communication and love my friends and family encourage
But their words only remind me that I don't possess enough courage
While I feel momentary relief through their inspiration
I realize I need more than just conversation
I need the truth to set me free
I need the scales lifted so I can see
Their efforts are appreciated yet it's just not enough
Too much time has passed and the road ahead is too rough

But I got a feeling

Is overcoming even an option?
The fear inside says approach with caution
It says that there is a way to fix this
So I try any and everything to enjoy flashes of bliss
Through all my planning, plotting and scheming I'm still in the same
        spot
With every move that fails my hope begins to rot
But I'm addicted to trying
And so the ideas keep flying
Making me think that this will work this time
Everything is going to be perfectly fine
So with every failure I'm surprised
And so the answer isn't behind my eyes

But I got a feeling

As my hope evaporates
I create an alliance with hate
My attitude allows the situation to overtake my life
So I look forward to bonding with strife

Extinguishing any relationships that may be right
Using every little word or incident to pick a fight
Mad at the world for this burden I carry
I push everyone away because I can no longer tarry
Patience has been lost
I can no longer afford this complication's cost

But I got a feeling

So now I must turn to the two I've known since birth
The two that allowed me to make a home on earth
Their advice is always true and fair
Ever since they said tuck your shirt in and comb your hair
As I listened with expectation and relief
I just knew that I would finally be free from the beast
But this time it was different their words were hollow
And the lack of a solution was too hard to swallow
I was vexed and disappointed
Peace was all I wanted

But I got a feeling

Advice all wrong
But maybe the words of a song
Could brighten my days
Pain don't last always
But after all the songs end
The pain does not mend
And I'm still in the same place
With a tattooed tear on my face
That reminds me of the hurt
So every morning I put it on like a shirt

But I got a feeling

So I lay on the ground tarred and feathered
Unable to cope in this type of weather
Looking up to the sky
Saying with my lips and screaming with my soul – Why?
Why did this have to happen to me?
I simply want liberty
To do the things that I want to do
So my hurt and pain continued to stew
I'll just stay unhappy and depressed
I'll just accept this chaotic mess
I'll let all my hurt define me
No more dotting the I and crossing the T
My life will remain incomplete, unfinished
Self-motivation will never replenish

But I got a feeling

As I went on with my life I realized
I had a permanent demeanor that despised
Hatred had suffocated me
So much that I didn't know me
This can't be life, there's got to be more
There has to be something beyond the distant shore
Even though I'm trapped
My feet want to stomp and my hands want to clap
Hope is present still
And faith says I will . . .

Thank God! Thank God!

I have a feeling that everything is going to be alright
So now I stay on my knees and in God's word, the only way to fight

"Have I not commanded you? Be strong and courageous. Do not be terrified; do not be discouraged, for the LORD your God will be with you wherever you go."

Joshua 1:9 (*NIV*)

I was born in a box with a closed top
It was taped down by someone I could not stop
My mind is his playground
And from birth all he did was freely roam around
Pattering into my future
Saying this is very important and be with her
My life's principles were in his control
Causing me to take my four aces and fold
I can't tell you what was going on
I did not do anything wrong
He convinced me of my perfection
And everyone was under my subjection
We became the dynamic duo
But yet I could never be a hero
As time went on my partner became my master
I would follow him through pain and laughter
I enjoyed every moment that we created
Not knowing that I was being hated
I knew what I could do and never tried what I couldn't
I knew what I should do, but I wouldn't
My world was already formed
And I was happy to conform
Average or below average was good enough
Striving for excellence was too tough
Yet my allegiance had been set

I always knew what would happen next
I would stay in my box with him
Until a hole caused a light to shine in

Faith

A Dream

*"Hope deferred makes the heart sick, but when
dreams come true, there is life and joy."*

Proverbs 13:12 (*NLT*)

I remember it like it was yesterday
Standing under that tent as the spirit began to make a way
Someone got up and spoke the Word
A man that I had never heard
But I knew him from the League
As he spoke my mind, body and soul became intrigued
Terry Cummings a name I will never forget
Because of the impression he left

Something happened to me that day when I was twelve
I never knew what I wanted to do, but there I was given help
I wanted to be like Mr. Cummings preacher & NBA basketball player
From that moment on that was going to be my prayer
I didn't know how it was going to happen
I just knew it had to happen

As I grew my dream continued to transform
But I wasn't growing nor was I better than the norm
I couldn't really shoot and I wasn't that tall
If you looked at the kids my age you would say I'm too small
But that didn't affect my dream
Because I knew God did not go on what was seen

However as I continued to increase in age
God was moved to the background of my dream's page
No more did I want to be a preacher & NBA basketball player
But a NBA basketball player & a preacher

I said to myself some day I am going to be in the church
But I kept putting God third, fourth, but never first
The dream I had was no more
And everywhere I went I didn't get closer
Tryout after tryout I was rejected
Until rejection was expected

Like the prodigal son I remembered
I recalled the spirit of God moving on every church member
I remembered going after Jesus at fourteen
I recollected on the original dream
I recalled the joy and peace I felt in God's house
God's love would never reject me or leave me out
The time had come to realign my life's plan
To become a Holy Ghost filled man
After years of misdirection and mistakes
Following after a dream that was fake
I am here a man saved and filled with the Holy Ghost
With no discussion or debate about whom I love the most
Ready and willing to give my dream, no God's dream, to God
Knowing that he will take and make the dream because He is God
I may be running out of time to reach this dream
However things aren't always what they seem
God has taken over this ride
And placed Jesus by my side
The battle is not over, but I have won
And now my life will be Jesus' fun

Am I Ready

"I have been afflicted and ready to die from my youth; I suffer Your terrors; I am distraught."

Psalm 88:15 (*NKJV*)

Am I ready? Am I ready?
We always want something
We always need something
We want what we see
We need what we don't see
But are we ready for all these things
Do we really want to be kings and queens
Can we handle the responsibilities
Can we continue to be us with these new entities
Or will these things captivate us
While we keep making sacrifices for things without a fuss
Losing who we are with every possession
Omitting our integrity to embrace our obsession
Disregarding love to bask in infatuation
Being undisciplined to fully enjoy emancipation
Daily we continue to pay the ultimate price
Never thinking maybe I rolled the wrong dice
Am I ready? Am I ready?

So how can we be ready for anything when we are confused
Throughout our lives we have been abused
We have been mistreated
We have always felt defeated
We have been hurt by friends and enemies
We have lived our lives without serenity
But now we should be able to make the right choices
With advice from the wrong voices

Our conscience is supposed to guide us
But how when it has been smothered by distrust
Insecurity has disabled our confidence
So believing in anything that comes out of us is nonsense
Am I ready? Am I ready?

Since birth they've told us we have nothing
So since birth we've been running
Chasing after everything we don't have
Ignoring everything we do have
Basing our lives on the feeling of love from others
Ignoring the love of our Fathers
Forgetting to love ourselves
And slowly fall victims to lies and tall tales
The sweet savor of victory is unknown
Because of lyrics in a childish song
We lost love on a one way street
Just because we did not speak
And what would we say
Except continue to treat me bad I love you anyway
Am I ready? Am I ready?

After all this we must now make decisions
But we're looking at things with bad visions
Do I really want that
Or did somebody tell me I should want that
Do I need that
Or did somebody tell me I need that
How can I tell what I need in a dark room
How can I tell what I want when I'm living in a cartoon
Can someone lead me back to reality
Can someone turn off this TV
I can see now that I need some illumination
I can see now that I need some revelation
I need someone to pull me out of this mess

So I can see what I have in my chest
Cause my mind is playing tricks on me
But my spirit is my true identity
But are you ready? Are you ready?

Confused

*"The LORD will make you the head, not the tail.
If you pay attention to the commands of the LORD
your God that I give you this day and carefully fol-
low them, you will always be at the top, never at the
bottom."*

Deuteronomy 28:13 (*NIV*)

No matter, the emptiness remains the same
I have continued to flirt with the insane
Why am I here?
This secret was never whispered in my ear
I was not given a blueprint at birth
No map or guideline to assist in my search
In my youth I looked to my parents
Idolization made me see their transparence
I noticed their faults and miscalculations
I've seen their success and continuous salvations
As I rejected them I looked for someone worthy
An entity with a special authority
From celebrities to friends I dove into the abyss
Ignorant to what was amiss
Embracing lover after lover
Underneath a black and blue cover
Misunderstanding the purpose of human life
Completely oppressing myself to desire's tithe
There was no need for building the throne of man
Ignoring me to only transcend to the desires of a sinful human
Seeking blindly for an exit strategy
Only to realize I'm trapped in my made tragedy

I can not wrap my head around the idea
Sometimes I am stuck between love and fear
Each having the power to keep me in this ignorant subjection
Casting my vote only to realize there is no election
As I momentarily disappear into each feeling
I am bound to an eternity of kneeling
Never blessed with the strength to stand
Needing the spiritual desire to say "I can . . ."
I can love and only love
I can only be above
I can do anything
I can transform from a frog to a king

Fire

*"But if I say, "I will not mention him or speak any
more in his name," his word is in my heart like a
fire, a fire shut up in my bones. I am weary of hold-
ing it in; indeed, I cannot."*

Jeremiah 20:9 (*NIV*)

The pressure is too much
Why do I have to be clutch?
I've failed at so many things
How can I ever be a king?
I was born a mistake
And my mother didn't send me down a lake
My heart is pounding so hard
My life is not feeling this new card

Yet something is there
Causing me to discard what I want to wear
I'm consumed with it
Because of it I can't quit
It drives me to pay it forward
It transforms me into a hero when I'm a coward
I'm forced to speak
When my being has accepted defeat
I find strength in it
It is my landlord, I'm its tenant
I've paid my rent
But not with dollars and cents
With sweat, pain and sacrifice
And every temptation can only entice
Because it gives me the power to overcome
So now I stand and fight, not run

The pressure is just right
To bring out my passion to fight
Failing is not an option
So I've canceled Satan's adoption
My birthright was to be a leader
To speak and not let my people be mind readers
So I let the blood flow
And cover me from head to toe
I will not be unemployed trying to retire
But stand, act, declare and live in the fire

My Time

Psalm 39:5 (NKJV)

The time is not my time
This rhyme is not my rhyme
Money can never be my money
Some of you are sitting here thinking that's funny
The truth is I own nothing
But I want everything

I want it all
From the antique cars to outlandish shopping sprees at the mall
I want to be the person that everyone knows
I want to be the friend with no foes
I want my every wish to come true
I want salvation regardless of what I do
I want the power to rule the world
I want to dance and twirl
On any woman's heart with no consequence
I want the freedom to do things that don't make any sense
I want to take love and bend it to my will
I want to misuse wisdom just to satisfy a thrill
I want to take the essence of humanity and subject it to my perception
Take the power of truth and make it deception

The time is not my time
These words are not mine
I don't own anything, not even my life
But I'm not simply rolling dice

Depending on luck to get me through
Rubbing a rabbit's foot before I do
If I was in charge of anything things would go
The way I want them to go
My money doesn't double
I don't stay out of trouble
The time is not my time
This brain is not my mind

The time has come for change
But this new development is not embodied in a title or name
We often speak about changing the world, but not our community
We leave our houses, our blocks, our family
Trying to change the world
But destroying our world
Not understanding that a staircase consists of stairs
A change in the world comes from a community's cares
How can we look past the needs of our own?
Just so we can help someone in a different time zone
Our heart is consumed with helping others
But we ignore our sisters and brothers
To spread our love across the seas
Trying to erase the guilt with deeds
Our global economy is poisoning our communities
We've outsourced our giving to other countries

We are all still tenants in this world of our landlord
Whether we drive a Mercedes or Ford
We must pay rent
We must abide by the agreement
We were given this world to use
Not misuse or abuse
Living today like there's no tomorrow
So now our children will only have sorrow
But that's okay because we want what we want

So our lavishness is the way we flaunt
Platinum rings on fingers and gold chains on necks
Minds focused on what should we buy next
Can we appreciate what we have and where we're at?
Can we focus on our turn at bat?
Can we consider tomorrow's world?

The time is not our time
This rhyme is not our rhyme
Money can never be our money
Some of you are sitting here thinking that's funny
But we want everything
So we end up with nothing
We have no community
Because we're free
The time is not our time
But we must use it to save our souls, our people, our future and our minds

Depend On God

"My salvation and my honor depend on God; he is my mighty rock, my refuge."

Psalm 62:7 (*NIV*)

I depend on God
I depend on God
I depend on God
I depend on God

Like the clouds in the sky
He is my reason why

I depend on God
I depend on God
I depend on God
I depend on God

Like the birds in the air
He knows my every care

I depend on God
I depend on God
I depend on God
I depend on God

Like the lilies of the valley
I know He will provide for me

I depend on God
I depend on God
I depend on God
I depend on God

More light than the sun and moon
I know He'll return soon

I depend on God
I depend on God
I depend on God
I depend on God

Fresh Anointing

> *"But my horn You have exalted like a wild ox; I
> have been anointed with fresh oil."*

Psalm 92:10 (*NKJV*)

Jesus, Yes, Jesus I need you
The test and trials, only you can get me through
Come, come now and save me, set me free
I'm trapped in a cell of impossibility
With my sin I caused you torture and pain
But I know your love and grace sustains

Lord I need a fresh talk
A fresh word, a fresh walk
Lord I need a fresh anointing O Lord

Here I stand forced to smile
But the pain inside is getting stronger all the while
Holding back love, holding back tears
Forcing me to love all of my fears
Trying to do this on my own
The pressures of feeling all alone
O Lord come take my cares

Lord I need a fresh talk
A fresh word, a fresh walk
Lord I need a fresh anointing O Lord

Hear My Cry

"Hear my prayer, O LORD, listen to my cry for help; be not deaf to my weeping. For I dwell with you as an alien, a stranger, as all my fathers were."

Psalm 39:12 (*NIV*)

Hear My Cry, Hear My Cry
Lord, I've done wrong and my faith is weak
All I need is for you to speak
I know you will attend to my prayer
And in your Word I know you are aware

Hear My Cry, Hear My Cry
Lord you've been a shelter for me
A strong tower from the enemy
You will deliver me from the workers of iniquity
For you are the God of my mercy

Hear My Cry, Hear My Cry
Lord you're my defense
And with love you give me deliverance
And when God is for me
Who can be against me?

Hear My Cry, Hear My Cry
My soul is with lions
But with every breath my voice will be cryin'
I trust in you
And you will bring me through

Hear My Cry, Hear My Cry

You Are

"I am the true vine, and my Father is the husbandman."

John 15:1 (*KJV*)

You are, You are
You are, You are

You are the true vine
Your love is sweeter than any kind

You are, You are
You are, You are

You are the light of the world
Your blessings are like a sea of pearls
I look to you as I'm praying on my knees
I look to you to supply all my needs

You are, You are
You are, You are

You are the bread of life
Through you comes the way of the right

You are, You are
You are, You are

You are the only door
When the world knocked me on the floor
You outstretched your hand
And you gave me another chance

You are, You are
You are, You are

You are the good shepherd
You make a way to go upward

You are, You are
You are, You are

You are the life and resurrection
You gave your life for our salvation

You are, You are
You are, You are

I love you Jesus, I love you Jesus

Special Way

"I will give thanks to the LORD because of his righteousness and will sing praise to the name of the LORD Most High."

Psalm 7:17 (*NIV*)

Father I want you
I want you more today
Father I need you
In such a special way
Father I praise you
I praise you more today
Father I love you
In such a special way

Yes Lord I want you
Yes Lord I need you
Yes Lord I praise you
Yes Lord I love you
More and more each today

That's why I want you
That's why I need you
That's why I praise you
That's why I love you
In such a special way

Father I want you
Father I need you
Father I praise you
Father I love you
In my own way

The Curse

Jeremiah 17:5 (*NLT*)

I have stared at this curse every moment I've looked in the mirror
So I guess my father was a bad giver
Passing down something I never wanted
Yet with ignorance I flaunt it
Giving my child the same curse
Knowing she will carry it from birth
Like an addiction that she will never be able to kick
I gave her a problem she can't fix
This sin I wish I could destroy
But with an ignorant bliss I treated my life and her life like a toy
I never understood my actions brought death or life
The war of good and evil was not my fight
I disregarded the right or wrong
And I was lost in a love song
With each verse and hook a new life was born
But she is kidnapped and torn
Between two who are still bound by past acts
Turning feelings and desires into facts
She does not understand
And is never given a fair chance
And this curse grows everyday transforming her reactions to life
Preventing her from becoming a virtuous wife
This pain will become her friend
And my choice, her curse she will call her kin
But this curse I know so well, can it be defeated
Or is my ammunition depleted

Has my choice broke her with no way of repair
But she has inherited more than just my eyes, lips and hair
She has inherited my heart
And her love for me will never depart

This love maybe our strongest weapon
Giving us power to dismiss acceptance of oppression
With love I will seek a parental relation
With love she will step on hate's temptation
With love I will enjoy her presence from a distance
With love she will understand her father's importance
Love will cause me to continue to support
Love will cause her to block all negative innuendos of me with an
    indestructible fort
Love will cause her thoughts of me to be pure
Love will cause me to ignore accusations and be mature
Then one day we will stand face to face
With arms itching for one another's embrace
That moment will erase years of absence
And we will be lost in each other's presence
Then where will the curse be
Mad because now it is set free

The Other

"And the second is like, namely this, Thou shalt love thy neighbour as thyself. There is none other commandment greater than these."

Mark 12:31 (*KJV*)

No one does anything alone
The Mighty men of valor helped David obtained the throne
Rebekah helped Jacob become Israel
A butcher helped Joseph's dream become real
We've heard we need each other to survive
But more than that we need each other to feel alive
We can't go through this world in solitude
Each other is the greatest gift from God and there can be no substitute
A hug can not be replaced with a click of the mouse
Or the purchase of a house
The conversation of humans change lives
The longing for another's voice or touch never subsides

If I was to stand here and say
I am who I am because of only me and God today
My pride knocks out God and would leave only me
My interaction with others has transformed me to be

A child is born and cries for the reconnection with another
Who can blame a child wanting the love of a mother?
But what about Adam wanting the love of Eve
He had the world but he asked God to fulfill this need
This is the first prayer of man
The need for woman
Or another when God went to his throne
And left man alone

Have we forgotten his prayer?
And the answer given him and us with God's care
Now the world has grown from two to billions
Only to embrace the subjection and ignoring of millions
We've forgot that it takes a community to raise a child
We only know our neighbors through a smile
So after nine months we have adults
Submerging ourselves into desperate cults
Yet we go on as if everything is okay
And do things our way

If I was to stand here and say
I am who I am because of only me and God today
My pride knocks out God and would leave only me
My interaction with others has transformed me to be

But there is a message lost in the hustle
Like saggy pants that need a belt buckle?
A solution to our equation
We must change this internal segregation
Stop isolating this need for something more
Slowly burning your soul to the core
Destroying the indestructible
Replacing the irreplaceable
But with every moment of life you need to receive it
Every thought of life needs to believe it
Every action of life needs to give it
Every feeling of life needs a piece of it
But we enjoy the byproducts never the manufacturer
Ignore the lecture because of the lecturer
But can we be alive without this true love

If I was to stand here and say
I am who I am because of only me and God today
My pride knocks out God and would leave only me
My love for God and others is transforming me to be

Evaluation

2 Corinthians 13:5 (*NIV*)

Who are we?
What have we become? Are we not free?
Are we not blessed with the rights to vote?
Did we not change nigger to a joke?
But yet our identity was lost in translation
We are descendants of a great nation
That has accepted defeat with no war
We have become so passive our words are a snore
We have committed the greatest crime
Not murder, but stepping out of line
We do not expect better of ourselves
And enjoy the media's tall tales
That we're thugs and ignore the facts
That this world was built by the sweat of our backs
And work of our hands
Not to mention the extraordinary blueprints and business plans
Ideas that shaped millions of generations
Flowed through our mind's creations
In a search for the truth we've embraced liars
Drove cars without tires
And fell short of nothing because we set no goal
But we do have control
Not of ourselves, but each other
Chose stereotypes instead of love to evaluate one another
I guess the price of freedom is freedom
No knowledge, no understanding, no wisdom
We are just free
Maybe that's enough for you, but not for me

Security Code

Psalm 91:2 (*KJV*)

You know sometimes I often think I'm nothing
I mean it's better than thinking I'm everything
Shoot, I know pride can put you on your hands and knees eating
    grass
But have I made myself less than last
In my thirst for humility
Have I destroyed heavenly possibility?

But within fidelity
I find security

I believed there's more to life than walking on a beautiful coast
I'm saved, sanctified and filled with Holy Ghost
But throughout my being there are foot prints of inferiority
Subjecting me to a mindset of obscurity
Causing me to know I'm not good enough
So I collect all this frivolous stuff
Trying to fill this hole
Not comprehending I need God's goal
Does God really care about a house?
Or is He more concerned about me being a slouch?

But within fidelity
I find security

Advertising has convinced me of my needs
So I changed my prayer every time I hit my knees
What is in God is God
Am I going to make a golden calf or stretch out my rod?
So in God's faithfulness
I find my best
I move from almost to excellence
I can't strive to be nothing, especially not in God's presence
I can't continue to overlook me
And therefore diluting the God within me

But within fidelity
I find security

When They See Me

"How long will you simple ones love your simple ways? How long will mockers delight in mockery and fools hate knowledge?"

Proverbs 1:22 (*NIV*)

Everyday I make an attempt to define myself
With each step towards this I find myself
Struggling to stand when my people are falling
Trying to tempt me, but God's spirit keeps calling
Telling me what's right and wrong, positive and negative
Being my best to destroy stereotype's perspective
I know that if I can transform
My people can see a way out of this urban hip hop norm
A way out of just fighting for scraps
Taking millions to just rap about how niggers are Black

Can't blame everything on the hip hop community
We were given this misconstrued identity
They snatched our messages for change
And transformed them into our new slave chains
History has repeated
Our spirit and mental is being defeated
The battlefield has moved to the brain
Freeing our bodies to make us insane
Questions after questions with no raised hands
It is time for someone to stand

Limited options causing some to turn to discrimination and segregation
Separating us from ourselves creating a nigga nation
Divide and conquer has become a success
We have turned on each other and now we are stuck in this mess

In our hands is extraordinary
Throwing it away cause we started to believe the temporary
Messages in commercials, movies, videos, music and fables
Making can't our new commodity when we are more than able
How can I, you sit there and let this happen
While the demise of Black folk got our slave masters clapping
I can't change the world!
Cause I got to go out with my boys or my girls
Martin Luther King, Malcolm X, Harriet Tubman, Thurgood
        Marshall, Jesus Christ, they were world changers
We are just life strangers
Scared to succeed cause we might fail
Scared to object cause we might go to jail
Lost the will to stand
Now we are sitting with extraordinary in our hands

Everyday I make an attempt to define myself
With each step towards this I find myself
Struggling to stand when my people are falling
Trying to tempt me, but God's spirit keeps calling
Telling me what's right and wrong, positive and negative
Being my best to destroy stereotype's perspective
I know that if I can transform
My people can see a way out of this urban hip hop norm
A way out of just fighting for scraps
Taking millions to just rap about how niggers are Black

One

"For through the baptism of the one Spirit we were all formed into one body, Jews or Greeks, servants or free men, and were all made full of the same Spirit."

1 Corinthians 12:13 (*BBE*)

One flesh one heart one mind
One future one present one past one time
One love one vision one hope one house
One word not just expressed with the mouth
One moves through all the limbs of our body
One flows through all the people of our community
One connects nations with nations
But cannot succeed without participation

One picture is worth a thousand words
But one action can never go unheard
One gun shot can destroy a community
So why can't one act of kindness build unity
Why can't one act of sacrifice change the outlook of a neighborhood?
Why can't one display of affection make a bad relationship good?
Why do we continue to finish the race before the finish line?
We chase after mediocrity as if it committed a crime
And we see excellence every day
But we simply choose not to live our life that way
However excellence is still there offering us real change, real future
With only one picture
Yet we get more than one dance
To show we deserve more than one chance
We get more than one interview
To show the world the real you
So everyone waits for the opportunity that we won
To display the power of one

One flesh one heart one mind
One future one present one past one time
One love one vision one hope one house
One word not just expressed with the mouth
One moves through all the limbs of our body
One flows through all the people of our community
One connects nations with nations
But cannot succeed without participation
Can I get just one?

The Witness

2 Corinthians 13:1 (*KJV*)

We come into this place with a notion of God
Some ignore His power to transform a rod
But if we ask Moses he'll proclaim this to be the truth
If you can't take his word for it ask Ruth
She'll tell you God is forgiveness and dedication
How in His truth there is salvation
A witness opens the doubting mind of the confused
These witnesses many have ignored and misused
But there is a witness

A person who stands and knows
Sometimes not seeing, yet faith grows
Defense in the imaginary because of hope
Seeing a challenge with no fear to climb the straight slope
People say this person's word is false
But how can one ignore this person's thoughts
If we take their words just as opinions we've lost
Lost the will to believe
The will to receive
The will to understand
The will of a perfect plan
But there is a witness

Finding the errors of each word
Declaring these to be just stories is absurd
Reasoning with how, why, where He rose

People wanting to believe, but drowning in the mind's nos
Rejection of belief brings infatuation with fire
Ignoring true love to be captivated by human desire
But there is a witness

Enjoying the meaningless in the culture fad
Stepping over the good just to dance with the bad
Proclaiming the truth only puts me to sleep
But hell is only skin deep
The temporal is in control
And now we can't grow old
But there is a witness

The present is here
The future is near
Yesterday is lost
Now we have to pay the cost
Ignorance has caused us to ignore the witness' rant
In dismissing their hope we step into a dimension of Can't
We have no visions or dreams
I love my neighbor is now my neighbor is too mean
Change is inevitable
But the witness' words are unforgettable
Thank God for the witness

Concept

I've tried to think of an answer for the most basic question
But with every explanation there remains another question
These questions always lead to the original question
Never an answer but merely a suggestion
With no hint of a reasonable definition
So, I've placed this question in my oven and allowed it to slow bake
What is faith?

This faith concept has engulfed my mind
Never having limitations like age or time
But an eternal being living with me
Capturing me and setting me free
A moment of love that lasts for eternity
A feeling that goes beyond man's possibility
A word that brings action
A picture that can not be caught in a caption

The introduction to faith is a word
Accepted by ears that hunger for the Lord
With every sentence penetrating their heart
Suppressing the feelings of being torn apart
Adverbs and adjectives accentuating thought
To destroy the manuscripts that the devil has wrought
Pronouns and nouns bring the rising of goose bumps
Urging the body to get off its rump
Transitional phrases transformed into nourishment for the soul
Each bite satisfying the young and old

Faith is not just one thing
But more like a contract sealed with a ring
Integrity through sickness and death
Tenacity that causes stature through the tests
How can we define faith with our vocabulary?
With each word we ignore it's extraordinary

www.ingramcontent.com/pod-product-compliance
Lightning Source LLC
Chambersburg PA
CBHW071503030726
47593CB00003B/1120